CH

MILLBROOK ARTS LIBRARY

FLUTES, REEDS, AND TRUMPETS

by Danny Staples and Carole Mahoney

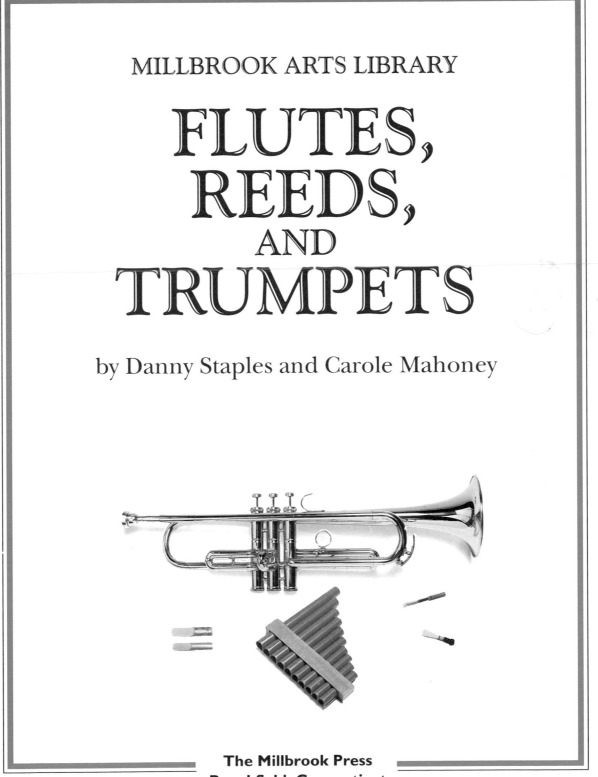

The Millbrook Press
Brookfield, Connecticut

Copyright © 1992 Merlion Publishing Ltd
First published in the United States in 1992 by
The Millbrook Press Inc.
2 Old New Milford Road
Brookfield, Connecticut 06804

Consultant: Denys Darlow F.R.C.M., F.L.C.M.
Designer: Tracy Carrington

Printed in the United States by Worzalla

Library of Congress Cataloging-in-Publication Data

Staples, Danny
   Flutes, reeds, and trumpets / by Danny Staples and Carole
Mahoney.
      p.   cm — (Millbrook arts library)
   Includes glossary and index.
   Summary: Explains and demonstrates how wind instruments work
and traces their development through various cultures. Includes hands-
on projects for making instruments.
   ISBN 1-56294-092-9
   1. Wind instruments—Juvenile literature. [1. Wind instruments. 2.
Musical instruments.] I. Mahoney, Carole. II. Title III. Series.
ML930.S78 1992
788'.19-dc20
                                        92-5165
                                           CIP
                                        AC MN

Cover photography by Mike Stannard.

Artwork on pages 9, 11, 19 and 33 by Kevin Kimber
and on pages 6, 8–9, 12–13, 22–23, 26–27, 35,
37 and 43 by Andrew Midgeley.

Models on pages 7, 9, 17, 21 and 41 by Tracy
Carrington.

Photographs on pages 4–5, 7, 9, 10–11, 12–13, 15,
17, 18, 21, 22–23, 24, 26, 29, 32–33, 34, 37,
38–39, 41 and 42–43 by Mike Stannard.

CONTENTS

Music from thin air

Musicians from the Mehinack tribe in Brazil

Take a deep breath and puff out your cheeks. Now blow out the air. Does the air make a sound as it rushes out of your mouth? It probably made a noise like rushing wind. You can make a louder sound with your breath if you blow into a tube.

Look around for some hollow objects. You could use a pen top, a hollow key, a straw, or an empty bottle. Place the open end against your bottom lip. Push your top lip out slightly, then blow over the hole. You should be able to produce a strong whistle. Experiment by moving your lips until you hear a good sound.

You can also make a musical instrument using your breath and your hands. Cup your hands together as if you are holding a ball. Leave a small gap between your thumbs. Now rest your lips against the thumb joints and blow into your hands. Blow softly, then harder. Move your hands slightly until you get a rich sound like the hoot of an owl.

Musical vibrations

Do you know how blowing across a tube or into your hands makes a sound? When you blow into something hollow, the air inside the hollow container starts to vibrate.

Jaguar Playing a Shell Trumpet is an ancient wall painting from Mexico

Some of the vibrations escape from the container into the surrounding air and vibrate in waves, which we call sound waves. The waves travel to your ears, and these pick up the whistling sound.

People have been breathing into hollow objects to make musical sounds for thousands of years. The pictures on this page show that you can make music with almost any hollow object you find around you. The jaguar in the ancient Mexican wall painting is blowing into a large shell. And look back to the picture of musicians from the Mehinack tribe in Brazil. They are blowing into hollow pipes to make a musical sound.

Panpipes

According to ancient Greek legend, the god Pan had the horns, ears, and legs of a goat and the face and body of a man. Pan often fell in love. One day, he was chasing a beautiful nymph named Syrinx. The gods took pity on Syrinx, and turned her into a reed so that she could escape from the god. Of course, Pan could not find her among so many reeds, but he cut one to remind him of Syrinx. Later, Pan made the reed into the first panpipes.

You can find panpipes in many parts of the world. They are a set of tubes of different lengths, joined together in a row. The tubes are usually blocked at the bottom.

A panpipes player from the Solomon Islands in the Pacific Ocean

Look at the picture of the musician from the Solomon Islands on the opposite page to see how to play the panpipes. As you blow, you move the panpipes backward and forward in front of your mouth to make different sounds.

Changing pitch

The panpipe tubes make a specific musical sound called a note. Because each tube is a different length, it sounds a different note. A short pipe gives a high note, because there is less space for the air to vibrate in. We say that the length of each tube determines the pitch of the note it produces.

There is another way to change pitch. If you find an empty bottle you can demonstrate how to do it. First practice getting a note by blowing over the top. If you can't make a note right away, change the shape of your lips or the position of the bottle. Or try strong, quick puffs of air. Now put some water in the bottle and blow again. What do you notice about the note? Put some more water in and try again. Each time

you add water, you reduce the space where the air can vibrate. So, each time, your note changes to a higher pitch.

Make your own panpipes

You can make your own panpipes from plastic tubing. Ask an adult to cut your tubing into about six pieces, with each piece slightly longer than the last. Then block the ends of the tubes with modeling clay. Wrap tape around the tubes to keep them together in a line. You may want to paint or decorate your pipes. If you have difficulty blowing a clear note on your pipes, try cutting a piece out of the end of each one.

The didgeridoo

An Aboriginal
didgeridoo player

A long, deep, vibrating growl is followed by a gruff boom. A throttled scream is quickly replaced by explosive barks. High squeaks seem to mix with strange and muffled voices. And all the time there is the long, deep growl . . .

Listening to these sounds, you can imagine a magical conversation between animals, plants, wind, sky, and the depths of the Earth. The music is hundreds of years old, and you would hear it in Australia. The sounds are made on a didgeridoo. Say the word slowly, didg-er-i-doo. The word sounds like the music. The didgeridoo is played by the Aboriginal people on special occasions, to accompany dancing.

A special instrument

Everything about the didgeridoo is fascinating. As you can see from the picture above, it is a huge instrument! A didgeridoo can be several feet long. And it is made like no other instrument. First a branch is chopped from a eucalyptus tree and may be buried in a termite hill. The termites eat the soft wood inside the branch, leaving a hollow cylinder. This is taken out, cleaned, and sometimes decorated with patterns. The patterns usually take the form of dream-like animals, whose lives are described in Aboriginal myths. Didgeridoo music often expresses the voices of these mythical animals.

Blowing a continuous note

Didgeridoo music is a series of almost continuous notes. It seems as if there is no time for the musicians to breathe. So how do they manage? The Aboriginal player has developed a technique of continuous breathing. It takes an incredible amount of skill and practice. Take a deep breath through your nose. Breathe out steadily through your mouth. Just before you run out of breath, puff out your cheeks. And then – this is the difficult part – squeeze the air out of your cheeks and take a quick, deep breath through your nose at the same time. It seems impossible, but there is no magic to it – just technique and practice. But you don't just blow into the didgeridoo. It's really a kind of trumpet. You have to start the air vibrating inside by pursing your lips together as you blow.

Make your own didgeridoo

Make an instrument like a didgeridoo from a long cardboard tube, or a section of plastic tube used for drainpipes. Your tube needs to be about 5 feet (1.5 meters) long. Decorate the tube with bright patterns and start practicing your continuous breathing! Once you can make the basic booming note, start experimenting. Make other sounds in the tube, like clicking, shouting, buzzing, croaking, and humming. You probably won't master the skill of continuous breathing, but you will make some good sounds.

Whistles and duct flutes

A Japanese whistle player

Do you have a whistle at home? If you have, you know that it is a narrow pipe topped with a special part to blow into, called a mouthpiece. Just below the mouthpiece there is a narrow hole cut out of the pipe. When you blow into the mouthpiece, the air is aimed right onto the sharp edge of the hole. This makes it easier to blow a clear note. Whistles with this narrow hole cut into them are also known as duct flutes.

Duct flutes made from many different materials are found all over the world. The picture on the left shows a very old Japanese flute from the 900s that is made from bamboo. Most modern whistles, like the ones below, are made from metal, plastic, or wood, but whistles can be made from bone or clay.

Modern wood, plastic and metal whistles and recorders

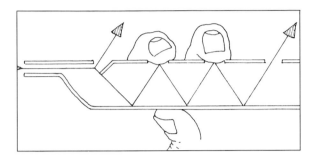

The passage of air inside a whistle with finger holes

Finger holes

You already know that to change the pitch of a note, you need to change the length of the tube. If you look at the diagram above, you will see that you can also change the pitch by adding finger holes to your tube. When you cover all the holes with your fingers, the tube is long. The air travels right down the length of the tube. When you cover only the lower holes, you are letting some of the air escape higher up the tube, so the tube is shorter and the note is higher. When you leave all the holes open, the air escapes out of the first hole it reaches, and the note is higher still.

Different shapes

Not all whistles have long, straight tubes. Many are small and have a rounded shape. You may have a toy whistle with a round body and a straight piece to blow through. The referee's whistle on the right has a piece inside it that rotates to give a better sound.

Ocarinas

An ocarina is a small whistle with finger holes and a rounded body. Ocarinas come from Portugal and are popular in South America, where they are often made of clay molded into interesting shapes like birds or people. The metal ocarina in the picture below comes from India. It has a chain attached to it so that you can wear it as a piece of jewelry.

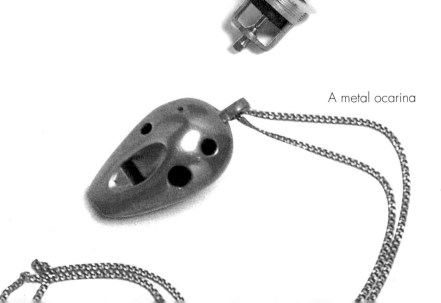

A referee's whistle

A metal ocarina

The story of the recorder

Arnold Dolmetsch

Late one evening in 1919, the Dolmetsch family joined a huge crowd of people waiting for a train at Waterloo Station in London, England. The family was returning home from a concert at which they had performed. Inside one of their bags was an old kind of duct flute called a recorder. At that time, recorders were rare instruments.

Seven-year-old Carl Dolmetsch put the bag down to rest his arms. Just then, the platform gates opened and the crowd of travelers surged forward. It was only when the train left the station that Arnold Dolmetsch discovered that his son had left the bag on the platform! The rare recorder was lost!

Are you wondering what happened to the recorder that was lost at Waterloo Station? Well, many years later it was found for sale in a junk shop. It was returned to the Dolmetsch family. And Carl, the seven-year-old who lost it? He grew up to be a talented musician and craftsman.

Arnold Dolmetsch set about making a new recorder in his workshop. Fortunately, he had made careful drawings and measurements of the old recorder. But it took a long time before Arnold was satisfied with the new instrument. He decided to make more recorders so that more people could learn to play them. The Dolmetsch family set up production in a factory. By the 1930s, the recorder was becoming as popular an instrument as it had been 200 years before.

A bass recorder

A group of
musicians playing
recorders in the
1600s

Sopranino, descant,
treble, and tenor
recorders

In and out of favor

When the recorder was a fashionable
instrument in Europe, composers wrote
pieces of music especially for groups of
recorder players. Then musical fashions
changed. Composers began writing
music for larger and larger orchestras.
Audiences enjoyed listening to dramatic
music in large concert halls. But the
recorder was not suited to large places –
it is best suited to small, intimate musical
gatherings where its gentle sound can be
appreciated. So people stopped playing
and making recorders.

Today, the recorder is popular again,
thanks largely to the Dolmetsch family.
Recorders are not too expensive to buy
or difficult to learn to play, so they are a
good instrument for young people to
choose. As you can see from the pictures
on these pages, recorders come in
different sizes. The large recorder is the
bass, which plays the low notes. The
smallest is the sopranino, which plays
the highest notes.

The modern concert flute

This picture, *A Flute Concert at Friedrich the Great's Palace,* was painted by Adolphe von Menzel

Many flutes are held sideways across the player's mouth. They are called side-blown or transverse flutes. The player blows across the top of a blow hole to play the instrument. Flutes are an ancient kind of instrument that became popular in European concert music about 200 years ago. Early flutes, like the ones in the picture on this page, had open holes along the pipe. You closed these with your fingers to change the pitch, just like a whistle. But early flutes were not easy to play because the fingering was complicated.

Making the fingering easier

A German jeweler and goldsmith named Theobald Boehm found an answer to this problem. Boehm was also an enthusiastic flute player, and around 1830, he concentrated his skills on improving the design of the concert flute. He wanted to make the complicated fingering easier. He invented an intricate system of keys, pads, hinges, and levers to cover and uncover the holes. This made the fingering much easier.

A modern
concert flute

If you look at the pictures of concert flutes on this page, you will see how Boehm's system helps the flutist. It means that the player can press a lever and cover more holes than would be possible with the fingers. So the skilled flutist can play intricate music easily!

Different flutes

Some flutists prefer the sound of a wooden flute, but most concert flutes are now made from metal. There are two other kinds of metal flutes that are larger than the concert flute and play lower notes. They are called the bass flute and the alto flute and are usually played in quiet pieces of music, where their mellow sound can be heard best.

An Indian
flutist

If you listen to *The Magic Flute*, an opera by the Austrian composer Wolfgang Amadeus Mozart, you will hear a concert flute played to great effect. It is used to mimic the sound of panpipes played by one of the main characters, Papageno.

The piccolo

The concert flute has a small relative. It is half the size and plays twice as high. It is called the piccolo flute, because piccolo means small in Italian. The piccolo has the same system of keys as the concert flute. You can hear the piccolo in the *Nutcracker Suite*, which was written by the Russian composer Peter Tchaikovsky.

An orchestral
flutist

Natural trumpets and horns

Early trumpets and horns were traditionally made from wood, animal horn, clay, or bone. The long trumpet in the picture comes from Tibet. It is so long that the player has to rest the cone-shaped end in a forked tree to play it! The picture below shows a natural horn from Africa. It is made from an antelope's horn.

Musical shells

Long ago, people discovered that some giant seashells were excellent ready-made trumpets. In parts of India, a trumpet made from a conch shell like the one in the picture on the right is blown at Hindu festivals. In the Pacific islands of Fiji, the largest shell of all, called a triton, is blown to announce the opening of the local fish market.

A long trumpet from Tibet

Early trumpets and horns were made out of natural materials in just the same way as early pipes. However, unlike pipes, trumpets and horns have a thin end to blow through and a thicker, cone-shaped end to carry the sound out into the air. It's often difficult to tell the difference between an early trumpet and an early horn. Trumpets are usually straight, and horns are usually curved.

A natural horn from Kenya

Sound cones

Try this experiment to see why. Roll a large piece of paper or cardboard into a cone shape. Speak into the narrow end. Your voice will be made louder as it comes out of the wider, flared end. You have just made a megaphone. "Mega" and "phone" are Greek words meaning "large-voice." The cone-shaped end, called the bell, of a trumpet or horn pushes the sound forward, making it louder. We say that the bell amplifies the sound.

A conch shell

Playing the trumpet

You have to use your lips to force air into a trumpet or horn and produce a good sound. Take a deep breath. Tighten your lips together. Now force the air out between your lips.

You will hear a sound like a buzzing bee. That's the air vibrating as it is pushed out between your lips. It is this vibration that makes the sound you recognize when horns and trumpets are played. Use your cardboard trumpets to blow some loud sounds or shout across the room to your friends!

The modern trumpet

In 1939, a rare silver trumpet with a long, straight tube was blown for the first time in 3,000 years. It was a tense and exciting moment. The effect was shattering. The trumpet broke into several pieces! The trumpet was one of two discovered in the tomb of the Egyptian Pharaoh Tutankhamen.

A modern trumpet

A fanfare is sounded with long trumpets

Tutankhamen's trumpet, like animal horns and conch shells, could play only a few notes. It was probably used for signaling or for playing fanfares on special occasions. Have you ever heard the thrilling sound of a fanfare? In Europe they are still played on straight trumpets for grand ceremonial occasions.

Folded tubes

The modern metal trumpet developed from long trumpets like Tutankhamen's. Straight trumpets like the ones used to play fanfares have an extraordinarily long tube. You can imagine how this would get in the way, especially in a band or orchestra. To overcome this problem, modern trumpets have been folded up! Look at the picture of a modern trumpet above. You can see how long it would be if the tubing were stretched out. If you measured it, you would find that the tubing is 4½ feet (1.4 meters) long! Modern trumpets also have a detachable mouthpiece, which helps to carry the vibration from the player's lips into the tubing more effectively.

Keys and valves

Around 1800, trumpets were developed that had keys, like the ones on flutes. Many more notes could be played on these instruments. A very famous piece of music was written for a trumpet like this. The composer was Joseph Haydn, an Austrian. It is called Haydn's *Trumpet Concerto*. It's still very popular with trumpet players today.

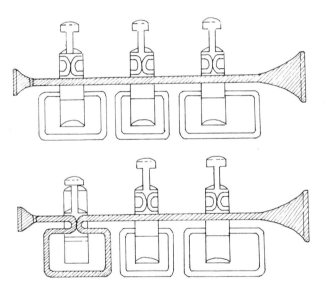

How trumpet
valves work

Valves

In 1815 an even better system was invented to improve the range of sound the trumpet could make. Three valves were added to the tubing. The diagram shows you how they work. When the player presses down on a valve, an extra length of tubing is opened. This makes a longer column of air and sounds a lower note. When the valve is released, the tubing closes again. At last the trumpet was able to join in and play any tune that had been written.

The trumpet certainly makes a stirring sound! It is probably most effective when it is played with feeling by a soloist like the American musician in the picture below.

A trumpet player at the Mardi Gras celebration in New Orleans

Modern brass instruments

The modern trumpet belongs to a family of metal instruments that we call brass instruments. The other main members of the family are the tuba, the trombone, and the French horn. When these instruments play together in an orchestra, we call them the brass section.

The tuba

The French composer Maurice Ravel decided to arrange a piece of music, *Pictures at an Exhibition* by Modeste Mussorgsky, for an orchestra. One of the "pictures" was of an ox cart lumbering along a muddy lane. He chose a tuba to represent the sound of the ox cart.

An Australian tuba player

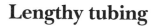

Lengthy tubing

The picture on the left shows you just what a large instrument the tuba is. Normally, tubas play the lowest notes of all the brass instruments in the orchestra. So you can imagine how much tubing it has – at least 12½ feet (3.75 meters)! In the early 1900s, an enormous tuba was built in America. The length of its tubing was 34 feet (10.36 meters)! It was so large, a person could disappear inside the bell. Tubas have the same valve system as trumpets.

The brass section of a modern orchestra

The trombone

A long time ago, the trombone was called the sackbut. It was named after an old French word "saqueboute" meaning "pull-push." Instead of having valves to change the length of the tube, like other brass instruments, trombones have a moving length of tubing called a slide. As you play the trombone, your arm does a "push-pull" action to move the slide in and out, making the passage of air longer and changing the pitch of the note you play.

The French horn

Even though it is a smaller instrument, the French horn has about the same length of tubing as a tuba. The tubing is curled in a tight circle. You can make an instrument similar to the French horn. You need about 13 feet (4 meters) of rubber hose, with a plastic funnel. Use a brass instrument mouthpiece to blow into. Curl the hose around and tuck it under your arm to play it. Remember to tighten or slacken your lips as you blow.

Brass bands

Can you imagine the sound of lots of brass instruments all playing together? Think of a band of musicians turning the corner and marching down your street! They are playing trombones, trumpets, and horns, not to mention cornets and tubas, as well as drums and crashing cymbals. You would probably see the trombone players first. They often lead a parade, so that there is plenty of space for their long slides to move in and out.

A trombone

A cornet

Special instruments

Brass bands have several of their own special brass instruments, which you wouldn't normally see in an orchestral brass section. One of these is the cornet.

As you can see from the picture on the left, a cornet looks like a small trumpet. But cornets make a much softer and sweeter sound. That's why they are used in brass bands instead of the more piercing trumpet.

The horns, too, are different from the horns in the orchestra. In 1845, a Belgian instrument maker named Adolphe Sax made a family of instruments called saxhorns, especially for use in brass bands. They are not called saxhorns now – their names are flugelhorn, tenor horn, baritone horn, and the largest one is the euphonium.

A Salvation
Army band

Playing together

Since the middle of the 1800s, brass bands have become an especially popular form of entertainment in many countries. In the United States, town parades always feature a brass band, usually with marching majorettes.

A marching band from England

In the northern parts of England, many towns and villages have their own bands, and many more are found in workplaces like factories and coal mines. Contests are held to find out which band is the best.

Since ancient times, armies have used brass instruments to carry out special tasks. They could be used for sending signals, such as "march forward" or "retreat." Their music would also keep up the soldiers' spirits and help them to march in time together into battle. Of course, army bands don't do this now, but they still play for special occasions and in parades.

Over a hundred years ago, in England, a man named William Booth started a different kind of army. His was not a military army, but a religious one. He called his religious group the Salvation Army. William Booth loved brass bands, and so he started his own to attract crowds to his open-air religious meetings. By the time he died in 1912, Salvation Army bands were playing all over the world.

Reeds

Have you ever made a shrill sound by blowing over a blade of grass held between your thumbs? As the blade of grass vibrates, it makes the air vibrate in sound waves. We hear the waves as a sharp buzzing sound.

Some instruments use a device that works in a similar way to the blade of grass to make a musical sound. We call them reed instruments. Reed instruments have a mouthpiece that contains one or two strips of cane, plastic or fiberglass. These strips are called reeds.

You can see different kinds of reeds in the pictures on this page. If an instrument has one reed in its mouthpiece, it is called a single-reed instrument. The two reeds at the top of the page are both single reeds. If it has two, it is called a double-reed instrument. Both the reeds at the bottom of the page are double reeds. When you blow into the instrument, the reed vibrates, making the air in the pipe of the instrument vibrate, too.

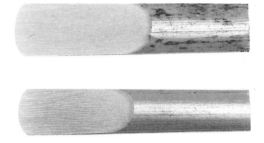

Double reeds

The two reeds of a double-reed instrument make an extra sound because they vibrate against each other. You can see how this works using a straw. Cut two slits in one end, then cut across the slits to make a wedge shape. Put the cut end of the drinking straw just behind your teeth, then close your lips around the straw. Squeeze the cut ends together with your teeth and tongue. Blow hard. You should get a vibrating sound. Now cut a short length off the other end of the straw and blow again. What do you notice about the pitch of the note? It should sound higher.

In a double-reed instrument, two pieces of thin reed are carefully cut, shaped, and tied together. The reeds are then fixed to the instrument. When you blow through the reeds, they flutter rapidly together. This makes the air in the instrument vibrate.

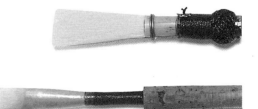

The shawm

Shawms like the one being played in the picture below are loud, double-reed instruments whose raucous, penetrating sound is ideal for events like military parades and other ceremonies. Shawm players often puff out their cheeks for continuous breathing, just like the Aboriginal didgeridoo musicians. Shawm music is popular throughout the Islamic world. Shawms are also found in Africa, Europe, and south east Asia.

A shawm player from Chad in Africa

Orchestral reeds

There is a children's story from Russia about a boy called Peter, his grandfather, a cat, a bird, a duck, a wolf and some hunters. The story is special because it is told not just in words but in music too. Each character is matched to an instrument of the orchestra. Whenever you hear the instrument, you picture the character it represents. Three of the characters are played by reed instruments – the clarinet, the oboe, and the bassoon. These are the three main reed instruments in the orchestra.

The clarinet

The sleek, black cat is played by the clarinet, which is a single-reed instrument. You can see a picture of one on the left. The clarinet can jump easily from high to low notes, play very loudly or very quietly, and move fast or slow. The low sounds are rich and velvety, the high ones piercing and bright.

A clarinet plays the sound of the cat

The oboe

The quacking duck is played by the oboe. The oboe can move very quickly from sound to sound, too. Its low sounds are raucous and reedy, its high ones thin and penetrating. This is possible because the oboe has two reeds that vibrate against each other, exactly like the shawm. The instrument on the right is an oboe.

An oboe plays the quacking duck

Peter's grandfather
is played by
the bassoon

A bassoon player
in an orchestra

The bassoon

The bassoon's tubing is four times as long as that of the oboe. The tube is so long, in fact, that it is folded, like most of the brass instruments. As you can see from this picture, the bell points upward above the player's head rather than down. It makes a lower sound than the other reed instruments. People say that some of its notes can sound like the human voice. Perhaps that's why the bassoon plays the voice of Peter's grumbling grandfather.

The story and its music were written in 1936 by a Russian composer named Sergei Prokofiev. It is called *Peter and the Wolf*. Perhaps you can find a recording of it and listen to what happens in the story. Do you think Prokofiev chose the right instruments for his characters?

All the characters
from *Peter and
the Wolf*

Jazz

Jazz is a mixture of many different kinds of music. Although jazz is now played nearly all over the world, its true "home" is the United States. This is where jazz began almost 100 years ago. Early jazz was created by black-American people, the descendants of slaves who were brought from Africa. Their jazz was a combination of a kind of sad folk music called blues, mixed with melodies and rhythms from African music, church music, brass band music, and from popular dances.

This early music is sometimes called Dixieland Jazz. "Dixie" is an area of the southern states of the United States. A band playing this traditional jazz is often made up of brass instruments like a cornet and trombone, with perhaps a clarinet.

Improvised jazz

Jazz is different from most other kinds of music. It is mostly improvised. This means that musicians make up the music as they play.

A modern American jazz band

The American jazz saxophone player Charlie Parker

Improvised music works best with small groups, where the musicians can easily follow each other. But large orchestras can play jazz too. These big bands were a popular form of entertainment between the 1930s and the 1950s. One famous band leader was Duke Ellington. He wrote his own music for his band and arranged it so that each musician knew what to play. Then during the performance, certain musicians played improvised solos on their own. The sound of big-band music helped jazz become known to a larger audience, and become popular in many countries outside the United States.

The saxophone

It was during the time of the big bands that the saxophone became such an important jazz instrument. Compared to other brass instruments, the saxophone is quite new. It is a single-reed instrument and was invented by Adolphe Sax, who you read about on page 22, about 150 years ago.

If you look at the picture of a saxophone on the right, you will see that it has a system of keys, like the keys of a concert flute. The saxophone, or sax as it's often called, is a very expressive instrument. Players develop their own personal style of playing. You can often recognize a particular musician after hearing only a few notes. A saxophone player with a good technique can play loudly or softly.

One of the most famous saxophone players was the American musician Charlie Parker. He helped start a new style of improvised jazz called be-bop. This jazz can be difficult music to listen to, but it is powerful and exciting.

A saxophone

Bagpipes

This painting, by the Flemish artist Pieter Breughel the Elder, is called *Peasant Dance*

Look at this painting of people noisily enjoying themselves. It was painted 400 years ago by a Flemish artist named Pieter Breughel. A man and woman are running to join in the dancing at a village festival. Around a table sit three men arguing. Children play. And what is the instrument that is playing music to accompany the lively dancing? It's an instrument called the bagpipes.

This instrument originated in the Middle East, but many parts of Europe and Asia now have their own particular form of bagpipe. The most famous type are the highland pipes, which originally came from Scotland. These impressive instruments, with their loud, forceful sound, are now played by musicians in many different countries around the world.

Bagpipes from Russia

vibrate, the player can breathe and still produce a continuous sound.

Not all bagpipes produce loud sounds. The Northumbrian "small-pipes," shown in the picture below, play enchanting music with a much gentler sound. They are not blown by mouth, but by bellows, which the player pumps by moving the arm up and down.

How to play the bagpipes

Bagpipes are very difficult instruments to play well. There are so many different things for the musician to do. The player has to blow hard into the bag and then squeeze it to push the air back out. At the same time, he fingers the holes in the pipe, or chanter, to play the tune. And then there are the drones, those long pipes that rest on the musician's shoulder. The drones make a continuous note that accompanies the tune played on the chanter.

Hidden reeds

Bagpipes are reed instruments, but you can't see the reeds. They are fixed in the ends of the pipes inside the bag. Usually a chanter has a double reed, like a shawm or an oboe. The drones generally have a single reed, like a clarinet. The bag acts as a reservoir for air. It is nearly always made of sheep's or goat's skin. You can clearly see the skin of the folk bagpipes in the picture above, although it is often covered with cloth. Because the air in the bag makes the reeds

Kathryn Ticknell, a Northumbrian "small-pipes" player from England

Free reeds

A modern mouth organ

Take a close look at the instrument in the picture above. It is called a mouth organ, or harmonica. This kind of instrument was invented in Europe about 150 years ago. Can you think how the mouth organ makes a musical sound? Each tiny hole has two metal reeds next to it, one short and one longer. When you blow into the holes, the reeds vibrate. Short reeds make high notes, longer ones make lower notes. These are called "free reeds" because they are free to vibrate up and down.

Playing the mouth organ

You hold the instrument so that the low notes are to your left. Try to blow just one single note by blocking the other holes to the side with your tongue. What happens when you suck? If you don't move your mouth, you will hear a different note. That's because you activate the second reed by sucking instead of blowing. You can see how it works by looking at the diagram.

The sheng from China

Mouth organs have been played in China for thousands of years, where they are called shengs. As you can see from the picture on the left, shengs are very different from the European mouth organ. They have long pipes, and each has a free reed inside. The sheng player blows and sucks air through a wind box to play the same note, with different pitches. The reeds vibrate when the holes are closed.

A Chinese sheng

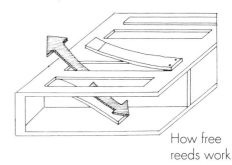

How free
reeds work

The American folk
and rock musician
Bob Dylan

Famous players

Some harmonicas are designed to play
very complicated music. One man who
became a virtuoso, or expert, on the
harmonica was the American musician
Larry Adler. He wanted to show that the
harmonica deserved to be taken
seriously as a musical instrument. The
English composer Ralph Vaughan
Williams wrote a piece of harmonica
music especially for Larry Adler.

The mouth organ is also an ideal
instrument for folk and blues music. It
has a mournful sound that goes very
well with a solo voice. The famous
American folk singer Bob Dylan is well

known for his mouth organ playing. Can
you see the frame he wears to support
his mouth organ? This frees his hands so
that he can play the guitar and the
mouth organ at the same time!

The melodica

The instrument in the picture below is a
melodica. It is a new kind of free-reed
instrument, invented only 30 years ago.
The body is made of plastic. The metal
reeds are controlled by a tiny keyboard.
Melodicas are cheap to buy and
easy to play.

A melodica

Squeeze boxes

Just like the mouth organ, a squeeze box makes music using free reeds. The largest squeeze boxes are the accordion and the melodeon. Musicians usually carry these instruments on a strap around their shoulder to support the weight. Squeeze boxes have three important parts. They are the reeds, the keys or buttons, and the bellows.

The bellows

The bellows are like a folded-up bag. The player opens and closes the bellows-bag with a push-and-pull action of the left arm. When the bellows are opened, air is sucked in, and when the bellows are shut, the air is pushed out.

Playing the accordion at the Moscow folk festival in Russia

A melodeon

The air flows past the reeds, making them vibrate and creating a sound. The player's right hand picks out the tune on a keyboard. The left hand presses groups of buttons at the other end of the bellows. On some accordions, there are as many as 120 buttons that can be pressed to sound chords. Each key and button controls a valve that supplies air to a reed or set of reeds.

The harmonium

You have to be athletic to play the harmonium! It is a free-reed instrument with a keyboard like a piano. It works in the same way as a harmonica and an accordion, the difference being in the way the bellows are operated. To play the harmonium, you have to pump two large pedals at the base of the instrument with your feet to fill the bellows with air. If you stop pumping, no noise will come out of the instrument. Small harmoniums that are pumped by hand are popular in India.

A harmonium player from India

Changing the sound

The keys and buttons on an accordion are called registers and complers. They can change the sound of the instrument completely. They allow one accordionist to sound like a whole group of musicians!

The concertina

Some squeeze boxes have different kinds of keyboards. A concertina is smaller than an accordion and is held in the hands with straps at each end. Both ends are hexagonal-shaped and both ends have buttons. Concertinas were traditionally used at sea to accompany sailors' songs called sea chanties.

The organ

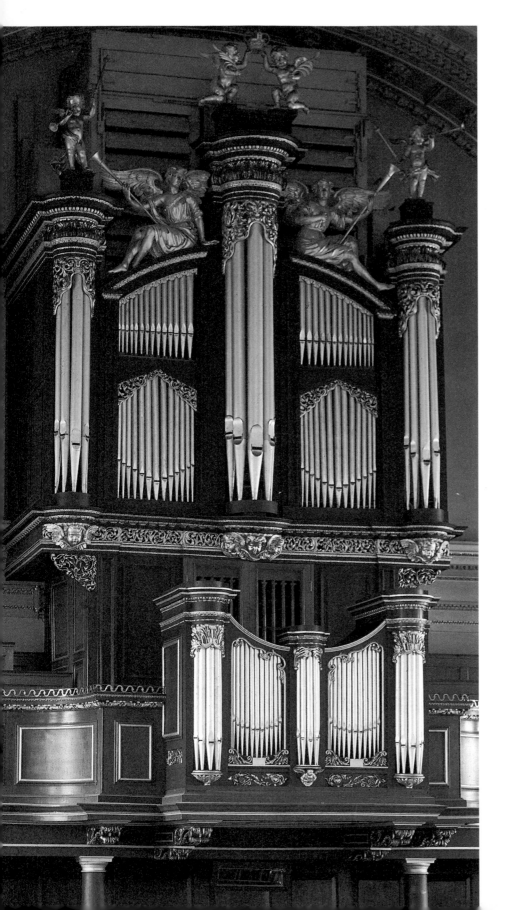

This picture shows a beautiful example of one of the largest of all wind instruments. It is an organ. Just imagine how much air is needed to make all these organ pipes sound!

Of course, people don't blow into organ pipes. Mechanical gadgets such as bellows and electric motors are used. In the very first organs, made in Ancient Greece and Rome over 2,000 years ago, water was used to force air through the pipes. The first organ was called a hydraulis, from the Greek words for "water" and "pipe." According to writers of the time, the sound was so powerful it could be heard many miles away, and the players had to plug their ears!

A few hundred years later, bellows took over the job of supplying the air. A monk living in England about 1,000 years ago tells of a gigantic organ with 400 pipes that sounded like thunder. It had 26 bellows and needed 70 people to work them! Today, only one musician is needed to play an organ even as large as this one.

The sound of pipes

The types of organs that still exist today were first used about 300 years ago in European churches. They are able to imitate the sounds of many instruments of the orchestra – the violin, flute, trumpet, oboe, and clarinet for example. Some of the pipes have ducts cut into them and work just like a recorder. Other pipes have metal reeds that vibrate like those of the clarinet.

A portative
organ

An organ pipe

Small organs

Not all organs were as big as this. The
small, sweet-sounding portative organ
was popular during the 1400s and 1500s
in Europe. It could be held and played
at the same time by one person. One
hand worked the bellows, the other
hand played the keyboard in the same
way as the Indian harmonium player on
page 35.

An organ's
keyboard and stops

Choosing the sound

The organist chooses different sounds
by pressing down or pulling out stops, to
open and close the pipes. Most organs
have two keyboards, called manuals, for
the hands, and one keyboard for the
feet, called a pedalboard. Each keyboard
controls a separate set of pipes. The
organist plays tunes on the keyboards
and operates the stops at the same time.
Eyes, ears, hands, feet, and brain all have
to work together to control such a
complicated machine.

One of the greatest composers for the
organ was Johann Sebastian Bach. He
lived and worked in Germany in the
1700s. When he was young he once
walked over 186 miles (300 kilometers)
to hear a famous organist play. Perhaps
this inspired him to write the organ
music for which he became famous and
which is still popular today.

Electrifying music

An electric
Hammond organ

Electric organ

The American inventor Laurens Hammond invented the electric organ in the 1930s. The electric organ looks just like an ordinary pipe organ, but doesn't work unless it's switched on. When the keys are pressed, electric signals are made. The signals go to a pre-amplifier, where they are made stronger, then to an amplifier, and then come out of the loudspeaker as musical notes. It sounds just like the real thing!

Electric pianos, like the one in the picture below, are popular with rock and pop musicians. It's a lot easier to carry a small electric keyboard around than a piano. The next time you hear some pop music on the keyboard, see if you can hear whether it's a real or electric piano.

An electronic
keyboard

When is an organ not an organ? Perhaps when it's electric. In 1937, the members of the Federal Trade Commission in the United States couldn't make up their minds. Could an electric organ really be called an organ? To decide the matter, they set up a test. One hidden player played a pipe organ, and another player played an electric organ. An audience listened and tried to decide which was which. They couldn't tell the difference between the two!

A musician playing
a synthesizer

The synthesizer

Shortly after the electric organ was invented, the synthesizer was developed. This machine produces a range of electronic sounds. It can sound like an organ or a piano, and it can reproduce sounds like the hooting of a car horn or the ringing of a telephone. Synthesizers don't always look like a keyboard. You might see some that need to be blown like a woodwind instrument!

Synthesizers give musicians complete freedom to experiment with sounds. They can perform any amount of complicated music single-handedly. Composers such as Karlheinz Stockhausen and Jean-Michel Jarre have written scores for electronic instruments.

Of course, you don't have to be a skilled composer to play electronic instruments – let the instrument do the work. In fact playing a synthesizer can be like having your own private orchestra. You can play pop, jazz, or even your own symphony.

Unusual wind instruments

Serpent

It is obvious how this instrument got its name! It looks like a snake, but it is not used by snake charmers. The serpent was first made about 400 years ago in France but is seldom played today. If the serpent were straightened out, it would be about 8 feet (2.5 meters) long. Remember the brass instruments whose tubing was so long it had to be folded up? A similar thing has happened with the serpent, but it is made of wood, that is difficult to bend. So it's made in short hollowed-out sections that are glued together. They are then covered with leather to seal the joints and stop the air from escaping.

A serpent

Snake charmer's pipe

Can snakes hear? Can they dance? Snake charmers in India would have us believe so. They play a pipe called a tiktiri. It is made from two cane pipes, each with a single reed. The pipes are fitted into one end of a hollowed-out dried vegetable called a gourd. The player blows through a hole in the other end.

The sound is loud and shrill, but the snakes can't hear it – they don't have ears. So why do they rise out of the basket and sway or dance? The reason is that they don't like the movements of the snake charmer and rise up in anger. Perhaps they can feel the vibrations from the music, too.

An Indian snake charmer

Nose flute

Blow through your mouth. Then blow through your nose. Which feels stronger? Even though you get a more powerful sound by blowing a flute the normal way, through your mouth, some people use their nostrils. In Polynesia, where nose flutes are commonly played, the people think that air from the nose contains a person's soul and so has more magical power than breath from the mouth. Nose flute players like the Brazilian musician in the picture below believe that their music has special significance. Nose flute players usually block one nostril and blow into the flute with the other.

Bullroarer

You can make your own unusual wind instrument with a thin, rectangular piece of wood about 6 inches (15 centimeters) long and ⁴⁄₅ of an inch (2 centimeters) wide. The exact shape and size are not too important. Ask an adult to help you make a small hole at one end. Tie one end of a long piece of smooth string into the hole. Make sure it is tied on very firmly.

Hold the string about half a yard (or meter) from the wood. Twist the wood with your other hand. The string will start to wind up tightly. Now move into a large open space, and quickly swing the wood on the end of the string around and around your head. You will hear an unusual roaring noise. You have made an instrument called a bullroarer.

An Indian from the Amazon rain forest in Brazil playing a nose flute

Writing music

An illustrated music score from the 800s

Sharing music

We call people who write music composers, because they make up, or compose, music. They write down their musical ideas so that musicians can play the music accurately. They are using music as a form of language to share their thoughts and feelings with the people who hear their music. Composers work in different ways. Some composers use a piano to play parts of the music they hear in their heads before they write it down. Some write many versions, or drafts, of a single piece of music, changing it over and over again until it is absolutely right.

In the 800s monks invented a way of writing music down. Before that time all music was learned by heart, or it was forgotten as soon as it had been played. Look at this piece of music, which was written in 1420. You can see that it is not that different from modern written music. You might think that the colors and decoration make it more attractive!

A written piece of music like this one is called a score. Scores can be written for just one instrument or voice, or for many instruments or voices. If there is more than one part, they are written one above the other.

We know that the German composer Ludwig van Beethoven wrote like this because many of his draft scores still exist today.

Other composers work completely in their heads and write down their music only when it is finally shaped. The Austrian composer Wolfgang Amadeus Mozart worked in this careful way.

The German composer Ludwig van Beethoven

A modern score

Today, modern composers are writing scores in different, new ways. Composers such as Karlheinz Stockhausen from Germany use diagrams and pictures as well as notes to convey their musical ideas. This means that a modern score can look quite different from a traditional one. Part of this Stockhausen composition is in the shape of a triangle. Have you ever seen a piece of music like it?

But no matter how different scores can look, they all serve the same purpose. They tell the musicians what notes to play, the speed to play them, and even the mood the composer wants to convey. A written score allows the musician to achieve a performance that is as close as possible to the music originally imagined by the composer.

A modern composition by the German composer Karl Stockhausen

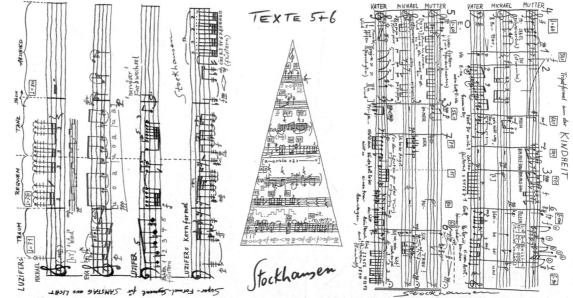

GLOSSARY OF INSTRUMENTS

accordion: a large free-reed instrument with a bellows bag joined by end keyboards. The accordion player uses a system of buttons to play complicated chords.

bagpipes: a pipe instrument with reeds that are sounded with air from a bag. The bag is inflated by air from the mouth or from bellows.

bassoon: a double-reed instrument with long, folded tubing.

clarinet: a single-reed instrument. Like the orchestral flute, it has the Boehm system of keys.

concertina: a small hand-held instrument with free reeds. Two keyboards with buttons are pulled and pushed to operate a central bellows bag.

cornet: a brass instrument that looks like a small trumpet. It is used in brass bands.

didgeridoo: a long, wooden wind instrument made and played by Aboriginal people from Australia.

duct flute: an end-blown flute that has a hole cut into it just below the mouthpiece.

electric organ: an organ without pipes. Sound is created from electric signals that are amplified and transmitted by a loudspeaker.

French horn: a horn with valves.

harmonica: a western free-reed mouth organ.

harmonium: a free-reed instrument with a long keyboard. The bellows are operated by hand or by foot pedals.

melodica: a modern free-reed instrument with a plastic body, a mouthpiece, and a small keyboard.

natural horn: an instrument made from a naturally curved cone-shaped object such as an animal horn.

natural trumpet: a naturally straight, cone-shaped object that has been made into an instrument. A large shell can be used as a natural trumpet.

nose flute: a flute that is sounded with breath from the nose rather than from the mouth.

oboe: a double-reed instrument developed from the shawm. The modern oboe has a system of keys.

organ: one of the largest wind instruments, an organ has pipes that are operated by air from bellows. It also has a complicated system of stops.

panpipes: a set of different-sized tubes fixed together. Blowing across the top of the pipes makes a musical sound.

piccolo: a smaller version of the orchestral flute, it sounds higher notes.

portative organ: a small organ that could be held and played at the same time.

recorder: a type of duct flute made from wood or plastic.

saxophone: a single-reed instrument invented by the Belgian instrument-maker Adolph Sax. Saxophones are popular jazz instruments.

serpent: a wooden wind instrument. Its long tube is folded into the shape of a serpent.

shawm: a folk instrument with a double reed. It is similar to an oboe.

synthesizer: a piece of electrical equipment that makes electrical signals into a wide range of musical sounds.

tiktiri: an instrument made from two or three pipes, each with a single reed, and an air reservoir.

transverse flute: a flute that is held sideways. The player blows across a blow hole in the side of the flute to produce a sound. The orchestral flute is a side-blown flute with a system of keys.

trombone: a brass instrument with a moving piece of tubing called a slide that is used to lengthen the tube.

trumpet: a brass instrument with a long straight tube or a folded tube. Modern trumpets have a system of valves to lengthen the tubing.

tuba: a large brass instrument with folded tubing.

whistle: a simple duct flute. Whistles can be made from clay, wood, plastic, or metal.

INDEX

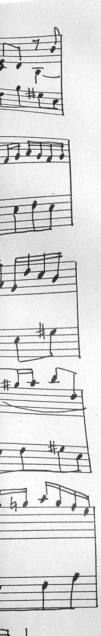

ACKNOWLEDGMENTS

The publishers would like to thank the following for permission to reproduce these photographs:

Ace Photo Library for Indian Snake Charmer (page 40). Axel Poignant Archive for *Jaguar Playing a Shell Trumpet* (page 5). Clive Barda Performing Arts Library for modern concert flute (page 13) and Karlheinz Stockhausen manuscript (page 43). Bridgeman Art Library for *A Flute Concert at Friedrich the Great's Palace* by Adolphe von Menzel, Staatliche Museen Press, W. Berlin (page 14); *Peasant Dance* by Pieter Breughel the Elder, Kunsthistorisches Museum, Vienna (page 30); organ case carved by Grinling Gibbons, 17th century, St. James's Church, Piccadilly, London (page 36) and The Old Hall Manuscript, polyphonic British Library, London (page 42). Collections/Brian Shuel for fanfare with long trumpets (page 18) and marching band (page 23). Compix/John Leach for Aboriginal didgeridoo player (page 8). John Guillaume for Australian tuba player (page 20). The Horniman Museum and Gardens for serpent (page 40). Hutchison Library for musicians from the Mehinack tribe (page 4); natural horn from Kenya (page 16); shawm player from Chad, Africa (page 25); bagpipes from Russia (page 31); Chinese sheng (page 32); accordion at the Moscow folk festival (pages 34-35); harmonium player from India (page 35) and Amazon Indian playing a nose flute (page 41). James McCormick Performing Arts Library for bassoon player (page 27). Redferns for trumpet player from New Orleans (page 19); brass section of a modern youth orchestra (pages 20-21); Charlie Parker (page 29); Kathryn Ticknell (page 31); Bob Dylan (page 33); electric Hammond organ (page 38) and synthesizer player (page 39). Sefton Photo Library for panpipes player from the Solomon Islands (page 6). Tibet Image Bank for long trumpet from Tibet (page 16). Werner Forman Archive for *Banquet and Concert* (page 12).

The publishers would also like to give special thanks to Emma and Helen Brierley, Merilyn Chambers, Kate Davies, Tim Gray and Mickleburgh Music Shop, Bristol, England for the loan of musical instruments.